CLA

SIMPLE, EASY, AND UNIQUE INDIAN RECIPES

By
Umm Maryam
Copyright © 2015 by Saxonberg Associates
All rights reserved

Published by
BookSumo, a division of Saxonberg Associates
http://www.booksumo.com/

A Gift From Me To You...

I know you like cultural food. But what about Japanese Sushi?

Join my private mailing list of readers and get a copy of *Infinite Sushi: A Complete Set of Sushi and Japanese Recipes* by fellow BookSumo author Hashimoto Kazuma for FREE!

http://booksumo.com/classical-indian-cooking-simple-indian-recipes/

Enjoy some of the best sushi available!

You will also receive updates about all my new books when they are free. So please show your support.

Also don't forget to like and subscribe on the social networks. I love meeting my readers. Links to all my profiles are below so please click and connect :)

Facebook

Twitter

Google +

INTRODUCTION

Hello, my friend. I would like to thank you personally for taking the time to purchase my book: *Classical Indian Cooking: Simple, Easy, and Unique Indian Recipes*. I truly do hope that these recipes are reaching you in the best of health and a period of happiness.

In writing this book I have taken the time to compile, what I believe to be, the simplest and easiest, classical Indian dishes into one source for those of my readers who are cultural food lovers.

After publishing my first book: *Arabia & Asia: A Cookbook with Recipes from Egypt, Morocco, Persia, & Pakistan* I noticed a strong interest in this type of food. So I made the decision to continue this cooking journey by focusing on a new country.

If you are interested in my first cookbook then please see the last few pages of this book where I've provided a link for where to find my seminal cookbook.

If you are interested in any specific type of food then please let me know. I'm very easy to find :)

In writing this book, I have tried to improve the style and content since my last cookbook. For each recipe, you will read in *Classical Indian Cooking: Simple, Easy, and Unique Indian Recipes* I've taken the care to provide not only ingredients with specific directions. But I've also tried to provide accurate information on the amount of time it will take to prepare and cook each dish, so you can plan accordingly before embarking on a specific cooking journey. Each recipe also contains information on its nutritional value as well as serving information. So for my health conscience readers check the caloric and fat contents of each dish.

I really want to provide the most value for you, my readers, so I figured this information will help a bit more. I'm constantly trying to improve and I listen to my readers. So please help me with feedback!

You'll find that many of the recipes require a lot of spice so make sure you have a lot of the following ingredients: coriander, cumin, yogurt, salt, pepper, cayenne, fresh garlic and onions, turmeric, and curry.

So without further ado, I will stop talking. Let's get our frying pans and food processors ready and take a trip to India with some simple and easy recipes!

Table of Contents

Introduction 4
Table of Contents 6
NOTICE TO PRINT READERS: 9
Legal Notes 10
Chapter 1: Simple, Easy, and Unique Indian Recipes 11
    Chicken Tikka Masala 11
    Makhani 14
    (Indian Butter Chicken I) 14
    Korma Vegetarian Edition 17
    Indian Style Curry Chicken 20
    Indian Curried Red Lentils 23
    Makhani 26
    (Indian Butter Chicken II) 26
    Indian Style Curry Chickpeas 30
    Spicy Potatoes With Curry 33
    Eggplant Curry 36
    Aloo Phujia 39
    Tandoori I 42
    Grilled Tandoori II 45

Tomato Chicken Indian Style 48

Korma 51

Spinach Dahl 54

Masoor Daal 57

Spicy Mango Chicken 60

Indian Style Eggplant 63

Aloo Gobi 66

Curry Shrimp 69

Curry Fish 72

Chicken Biryani 75

Brown Rice, Chicken, Curry, Casserole 80

Aloo Matar 83

Potatoes Indian Style 86

Dahl II 89

Okra Curry 92

Lentil, Tomato Soup, Indian Style 95

Indian Style Salsa 98

A Gift From Me To You 100

Come On 102

Let's Be Friends :) 102

About The Publisher 103

Can I Ask A Favour? 104

INTERESTED IN MY OTHER COOKBOOKS? 105

NOTICE TO PRINT READERS:

Hey, because you purchased the print version of this book you are entitled to its original digital version for free by Amazon.

So when you have the time, please review your purchases, and download the Kindle version of this book.

You might enjoy consuming this book more in its original digital format.

;)

But, in any case, take care and enjoy reading in whatever format you choose!

LEGAL NOTES

ALL RIGHTS RESERVED. NO PART OF THIS BOOK MAY BE REPRODUCED OR TRANSMITTED IN ANY FORM OR BY ANY MEANS. PHOTOCOPYING, POSTING ONLINE, AND / OR DIGITAL COPYING IS STRICTLY PROHIBITED UNLESS WRITTEN PERMISSION IS GRANTED BY THE BOOK'S PUBLISHING COMPANY. LIMITED USE OF THE BOOK'S TEXT IS PERMITTED FOR USE IN REVIEWS WRITTEN FOR THE PUBLIC AND/OR PUBLIC DOMAIN.

CHAPTER 1: SIMPLE, EASY, AND UNIQUE INDIAN RECIPES

CHICKEN TIKKA MASALA

Ingredients

1. One cup yogurt
2. One tbsp lemon juice
3. 2 tsps ground cumin
4. One tsp ground cinnamon
5. 2 tsps cayenne pepper
6. 2 tsps freshly ground black pepper
7. One tbsp minced fresh ginger
8. 4 tsps salt, or to taste
9. 3 boneless skinless chicken breasts, cut into bite-size pieces
10. 4 long skewers
11. One tbsp butter
12. One clove garlic, minced
13. One jalapeno pepper, finely chopped
14. 2 tsps ground cumin
15. 2 tsps paprika
16. 3 tsps salt, or to taste
17. One (8 ounce) can tomato sauce
18. One cup heavy cream
19. 1/4 cup chopped fresh cilantro

DIRECTIONS:

1. Take lemon juice, yogurt, two tsps cumin, cayenne, cinnamon, ginger, black pepper, 4

tsps of salt and add into one mixing dish (possibly a big bowl).
2. Add the chicken to the marinade, cover it, and place it in a refrigerator for one hour.
3. Preheat a grill or frying pan to its highest heat.
4. Add chicken to skewers and throw away the marinade.
5. Add some butter or non stick spray to your grilling grate.
6. Place the chicken on the grill and allow it to cook until its juices are clear. The approx. time is equal to about 5 minutes on each side.
7. Take your butter and place it into a big skillet or wok. The skillet or wok should be placed over medium heat.
8. For about one minute stir fry (sauté) some garlic and jalapeno.
9. Take some paprika and cumin (approx. 2 tbsps each), and also three tsps of salt and add these ingredients to the garlic and jalapeno.
10. Grab some cream and tomato sauce and place the two ingredients on low heat and continually stir the contents until they become thick. This process should take about 20 minutes.
11. Combine everything with your grilled chicken and let everything cook for an additional ten minutes.
12. Plate your contents and add some cilantro as a garnish.
13. Enjoy.

Serving Size: 4 servings

Preparation	Cooking	Total Time
30 mins	50 mins	2 hrs 20 mins

Nutrition Information:

Calories	404 kcal
Carbohydrates	13.3 g
Cholesterol	143 mg
Fat	28.9 g
Fiber	2.5 g
Protein	24.6 g
Sodium	4499 mg

* Percent Daily Values are based on a 2,000 calorie diet

MAKHANI

(INDIAN BUTTER CHICKEN I)

Ingredients

1. One tbsp peanut oil
2. One shallot, finely chopped
3. 1/4 white onion, chopped
4. 2 tbsps butter
5. 2 tsps lemon juice
6. One tbsp ginger garlic paste
7. One tsp garam masala
8. One tsp chili powder
9. One tsp ground cumin
10. One bay leaf
11. 1/4 cup plain yogurt
12. One cup half-and-half
13. One cup tomato puree
14. 1/4 tsp cayenne pepper, or to taste
15. One pinch salt
16. One pinch black pepper
17. One tbsp peanut oil
18. One pound boneless, skinless chicken thighs, cut into bite-size pieces
19. One tsp garam masala
20. One pinch cayenne pepper
21. One tbsp cornstarch
22. 1/4 cup water

DIRECTIONS:

1. Grab a saucepan (as large as possible) and heat it over medium heat.
2. Take some onions and shallots and stir fry them until they are soft and see-through. Combine onions and shallots with the following ingredients: one bay leaf, some butter, chili powder, one tsp of garam masala, ginger-garlic paste, lemon juice, and cumin.
3. For approx. one minute the ingredients should be stir fried.
4. For approx two more minutes continue to stir contents consistently and add some tomato sauce, some yogurt, and finally some half and half cream.
5. It is important that you continue to stir the mixture for an additional 10 minutes over low heat, letting it simmer.
6. Add some salt and pepper and place the cooking pot to the side away from the heating source.
7. Take another skillet and add one tbsp of oil over a medium level heat.
8. Add some chicken to your heated oil and cook it for about 10 minutes until it is lightly brown.
9. Grab some garam masala (One tsp) as well as some cayenne (same amount) and add it to the chicken, reduce the heat.
10. Combine 3 tbsps of sauce with the chicken and simmer the contents until your chicken is no longer pink.
11. Once the chicken is fully cooked (i.e. no longer pink) add it to the sauce.
12. Combine some water and cornstarch and mix it with the sauce. Allow everything to cook for an

additional five to ten minutes, until it is thickened.
13. Plate, serve, enjoy.

Serving Size: 4 servings

Preparation	Cooking	Total Time
10 mins	25 mins	35 mins

Nutrition Information:

Calories	408 kcal
Carbohydrates	15.6 g
Cholesterol	107 mg
Fat	27.8 g
Fiber	2.2 g
Protein	23.4 g
Sodium	620 mg

* Percent Daily Values are based on a 2,000 calorie diet.

Korma Vegetarian Edition

Ingredients

1. One 1/2 tbsps vegetable oil
2. One small onion, diced
3. One tsp minced fresh ginger root
4. 4 cloves garlic, minced
5. 2 potatoes, cubed
6. 4 carrots, cubed
7. One fresh jalapeno pepper, seeded and sliced
8. 3 tbsps ground unsalted cashews
9. One (4 ounce) can tomato sauce
10. 2 tsps salt
11. One 1/2 tbsps curry powder
12. One cup frozen green peas
13. 1/2 green bell pepper, chopped
14. 1/2 red bell pepper, chopped
15. One cup heavy cream
16. One bunch fresh cilantro for garnish

DIRECTIONS:

1. Grab your oil and add it to a skillet or frying pan. Skillet should be set over medium heat.
2. Combine with oil, some onions, and let it cook until completely translucent. Next you should combine: garlic and ginger.
3. Let the new mixture of cooked onions, garlic, and ginger, cook for approx. one minute.
4. Grab some carrots, cashews, potatoes, and tomato sauce, and combine them all with some curry powder and salt for seasoning.

5. Allow everything to cook for approx ten mins. taking care to stir consistently. Make sure that your potatoes are tender before moving to the next step.
6. Take the following ingredients and stir them into your current mixture: peas, green and red bell peppers, and cream.
7. Simmer everything for about 10 minutes on low heat.
8. Plate your dish for serving.

Serving Size: 4 servings

Preparation	Cooking	Total Time
25 mins	30 mins	55 mins

Nutrition Information:

Calories	462 kcal
Carbohydrates	41.3 g
Cholesterol	82 mg
Fat	31 g
Fiber	8.4 g
Protein	8.6 g
Sodium	1434 mg

* Percent Daily Values are based on a 2,000 calorie diet.

Indian Style Curry Chicken

Ingredients

1. 3 tbsps olive oil
2. One small onion, chopped
3. 2 cloves garlic, minced
4. 3 tbsps curry powder
5. One tsp ground cinnamon
6. One tsp paprika
7. One bay leaf
8. 1/2 tsp grated fresh ginger root
9. 1/2 tsp white sugar
10. salt to taste
11. 2 skinless, boneless chicken breast halves - cut into bite-size pieces
12. One tbsp tomato paste
13. One cup plain yogurt
14. 3/4 cup coconut milk
15. 1/2 lemon, juiced
16. 1/2 tsp cayenne pepper

DIRECTIONS:

1. Grab a large skillet or cooking dish. Place the pot over medium heat, let it get hot.
2. Add some oil to the pot and stir fry some onions until they are slightly brown and translucent.
3. Combine with the onions the following ingredients for seasoning: sugar, salt, ginger, one bay leaf, paprika, cinnamon, curry powder, and garlic.

4. Take care to continually stir these ingredients together over the medium heat for at least two mins.
5. Grab your yoghurt, tomato paste, coconut milk, and chicken pieces, add everything together, and let it cook until it begins to boil.
6. Once the contents begin to bowl lower the heat on the stove and let everything simmer for about 20 to 25 mins.
7. Add some lemon juice, and cayenne pepper and let it cook and simmer for an additional five mins.
8. Plate and enjoy.

Serving Size: 4 to 6 servings

Preparation	Cooking	Total Time
20 mins	25 mins	45 mins

Nutrition Information:

Calories	313 kcal
Carbohydrates	14 g
Cholesterol	38 mg
Fat	21.7 g
Fiber	3.8 g
Protein	19.1 g
Sodium	268 mg

* Percent Daily Values are based on a 2,000 calorie diet.

Indian Curried Red Lentils

Ingredients

1. 2 cups red lentils
2. One large onion, diced
3. One tbsp vegetable oil
4. 2 tbsps curry paste
5. One tbsp curry powder
6. One tsp ground turmeric
7. One tsp ground cumin
8. One tsp chili powder
9. One tsp salt
10. One tsp white sugar
11. One tsp minced garlic
12. One tsp minced fresh ginger
13. One (14.25 ounce) can tomato puree

DIRECTIONS:

1. Before you being, take your lentils, and wash them. Let water run over them until it runs clear without any traces of dirt or grime.
2. Grab a nice sized pot and place in lentils and cover them with water and get it all boiling, cover the pot and take its heat level to medium.
3. While your lentils are boiling you will have to add water continually to keep them covered. Cook the lentils until they are soft which will typically take about 15 to 20 mins.
4. Once your lentils are tender you should drain the pot.

5. Grab a large frying pan or skillet and heat it up over medium heat. Add some oil and onions and fry them until they are caramelized (possibly 20 minutes of cooking time, take care to ensure your onions do not burn).
6. Once the onions are caramelized combine the following ingredients for seasoning: turmeric, ginger, sugar, curry powder, cumin, chili powder, curry paste, and salt.
7. Increase the heat of the skillet and stir consistently until the ingredients begin to create a beautiful aroma, this will take about one to two minutes.
8. Combine your tomato puree with the seasonings and remove everything from heat.
9. Once removed from heat add your lentils and mix accordingly.
10. Plate, serve, enjoy.

Serving Size: 8 servings

Preparation	Cooking	Total Time
10 mins	30 mins	40 mins

Nutrition Information:

Calories	192 kcal
Carbohydrates	32.5 g
Cholesterol	0 mg
Fat	2.6 g
Fiber	11.3 g
Protein	12.1 g
Sodium	572 mg

* Percent Daily Values are based on a 2,000 calorie diet.

MAKHANI

(INDIAN BUTTER CHICKEN II)

Ingredients

1. One cup butter, divided
2. One onion, minced
3. One tbsp minced garlic
4. One (15 ounce) can tomato sauce
5. 3 cups heavy cream
6. 2 tsps salt
7. One tsp cayenne pepper
8. One tsp garam masala
9. One 1/2 pounds skinless, boneless chicken breast, cut into bite-sized chunks
10. 2 tbsps vegetable oil
11. 2 tbsps tandoori masala

DIRECTIONS:

1. The first step for this process is to preheat your oven to 375 degrees Fahrenheit or 190 degrees Celsius.
2. Grab a skillet and add 2 tbsps of butter. The skillet should be heated with a medium level of heat.
3. Make sure that your butter is fully melted and not burnt and begin to mix in some garlic and onions.
4. Fry your garlic and onions for approx. 15 to 20 minutes until the onions have caramelized nicely.

5. While you are frying your onions and garlic you should have another sauce pan with the remaining amount of butter present, heating over medium to high heat.
6. Once the butter has melted fully in your second sauce pan begin to mix in the following ingredients: tomato sauce, heavy cream, cayenne pepper, salt, and some garam masala. Allow everything to cook until it has begun simmering.
7. Once the second sauce pan is simmering lower the heat to a medium to low setting and cover the pan and let it simmer for 30 minutes. Make sure to stir the contents every few minutes.
8. Once the onions have caramelized fully add them and the garlic to the second saucepan.
9. Once everything has been combined and your sauce is simmering nicely make sure it is on low heat.
10. Begin to mix chicken cubes with vegetable oil and add some tandoori masala in a separate bowl.
11. Take some tbsps of sauce and add it to the chicken pieces to coat them evenly. Once the chicken has been coated with sauce, oil, and tandoori masala, spread each piece evenly over a baking dish.
12. Place baking dish with seasoned chicken pieces into the preheated oven and cook for at least 12 minutes or longer. Just make sure your chicken is fully cooked and no longer pink in the middle.

13. Once chicken is fully cooked, remove it from the oven, and combine it with the sauce and simmer for an additional 5 minutes.
14. Plate and serve.

Servings: ≈4 servings

Preparation	Cooking	Total Time
15 mins	45 mins	1 hr

Nutrition Information:

Calories	880 kcal
Carbohydrates	12.8 g
Cholesterol	303 mg
Fat	82.3 g
Fiber	2.6 g
Protein	26.4 g
Sodium	1461 mg

* Percent Daily Values are based on a 2,000 calorie diet

Indian Style Curry Chickpeas

Ingredients

1. 2 tbsps vegetable oil
2. 2 onions, minced
3. 2 cloves garlic, minced
4. 2 tsps fresh ginger root, finely chopped
5. 6 whole cloves
6. 2 (2 inch) sticks cinnamon, crushed
7. One tsp ground cumin
8. One tsp ground coriander
9. salt
10. One tsp cayenne pepper
11. One tsp ground turmeric
12. 2 (15 ounce) cans garbanzo beans
13. One cup chopped fresh cilantro

DIRECTIONS:

1. Grab a big skillet or frying pan and heat it over a medium level of heat.
2. Add some oil and onions to your pan and cook them down until they are tender.
3. While your onions are frying add the following seasonings: turmeric, salt, cayenne, garlic, cinnamon, cumin, ginger, and coriander.
4. Let your seasonings and onions continue to cook over the medium heat for about one to two minutes making sure to stir frequently.
5. Grab some garbanzo beans and the associated garbanzo bean liquid and combine them with the seasoned onions.

6. Mix and stir everything together and continue to cook until everything is well mixed and evenly heated.
7. Combine some cilantro to the mix and before removing everything from the heating source.
8. Plate, and enjoy. Garnish the food with fresh cilantro.

Serving Size: 8 servings

Preparation	Cooking	Total Time
10 mins	30 mins	40 mins

Nutrition Information:

Calories	135 kcal
Carbohydrates	20.5 g
Cholesterol	0 mg
Fat	4.5 g
Fiber	4.6 g
Protein	4.1 g
Sodium	289 mg

* Percent Daily Values are based on a 2,000 calorie diet.

SPICY POTATOES WITH CURRY

Ingredients

1. 4 potatoes, peeled and cubed
2. 2 tbsps vegetable oil
3. One yellow onion, diced
4. 3 cloves garlic, minced
5. 2 tsps ground cumin
6. One 1/2 tsps cayenne pepper
7. 4 tsps curry powder
8. 4 tsps garam masala
9. One (One inch) piece fresh ginger root, peeled and minced
10. 2 tsps salt
11. One (14.5 ounce) can diced tomatoes
12. One (15 ounce) can garbanzo beans (chickpeas), rinsed and drained
13. One (15 ounce) can peas, drained
14. One (14 ounce) can coconut milk

DIRECTIONS:

1. Get yourself a large pot and add some water, some salt, and your potatoes.
2. Place the pot and the potatoes over high heat and allow the contents to begin to boil. Once everything is boiling lower the heat to a medium to low level.
3. Cover the pot and let it simmer for some time until you find that your potatoes are tender (should take about 15 to 20 minutes of simmering).

4. Once the potatoes are tender remove the water and let the spuds steam dry for about 2 mins.
5. While the potatoes are drying grab a large frying pan or skillet and place it over medium heat with some vegetable oil.
6. Place some garlic and onions in the oil and being to cook until everything is translucent (should take about 5 minutes).
7. Now we want to season the onions and garlic with the following ingredients: ginger, salt, cumin, cayenne, curry, and masala.
8. Allow the onions and the seasonings to cook for another 2 two minutes or until you being to smell a great aroma.
9. Combine with the seasoned onions, your garbanzo beans, tomatoes, peas and tomatoes with some coconut milk and cook until everything is simmering.
10. Let the contents simmer for 5 to 10 minutes.
11. Let cool. Plate, serve, eat, enjoy.

Serving Size: 6 servings

Preparation	Cooking	Total Time
30 mins	30 mins	1 hr

Nutrition Information:

Calories	407 kcal
Carbohydrates	50.6 g
Cholesterol	0 mg
Fat	20.1 g
Fiber	10.1 g
Protein	10.1 g
Sodium	1176 mg

* Percent Daily Values are based on a 2,000 calorie diet.

Eggplant Curry

Ingredients

1. One large eggplant
2. 2 tbsps vegetable oil
3. One tsp cumin seeds
4. One medium onion, thinly sliced
5. One tbsp ginger garlic paste
6. One tbsp curry powder
7. One tomato, diced
8. 1/2 cup plain yogurt
9. One fresh jalapeno chili pepper, finely chopped
10. One tsp salt
11. 1/4 bunch cilantro, finely chopped

DIRECTIONS:

1. Before we can begin this recipe we have to first get our oven hot. So preheat the oven to 450 degrees Fahrenheit or 230 degrees Celsius.
2. Grab some eggplant and a baking sheet.
3. Put your eggplant on the baking sheet and let it cook in the oven for about 20 to 30 minutes. You will find that after this time the eggplant will be tender. If not let them cook longer.
4. Once the eggplants are tender take them out of the oven, let them sit aside to lose their hotness, peel them, and chop them up for the next steps.
5. Get a medium sized pan for sauce and add some oil. Heat the oil and the pan over a medium level of heat.

6. Combine onion and cumin seeds with the heated oil. Cook everything over the medium heat until the onions are translucent.
7. Combine garlic paste, ginger, tomato, and curry, in the pan and fry it for one min. Now you want to mix in some yogurt.
8. Now mix in the cool, chopped, and peeled eggplant, with jalapeno peppers and some salt for seasoning.
9. Allow everything to cook for about ten mins. Make sure that the pan is covered and everything is over high heat.
10. After ten mins take off the pan's cover, and turn the heat down to low. Let the food continue to cook for an additional five mins.
11. After five mins has elapsed the food is ready for serving.
12. Turn off heat. Garnish with cilantro.
13. Serve and enjoy.

Serving Size: 4 servings

Preparation	Cooking	Total Time
15 mins	45 mins	1 hr

Nutrition Information:

Calories	146 kcal
Carbohydrates	15.2 g
Cholesterol	2 mg
Fat	8 g
Fiber	6.2 g
Protein	4 g
Sodium	739 mg

* Percent Daily Values are based on a 2,000 calorie diet.

ALOO PHUJIA

Ingredients

1. One onion, chopped
2. 1/4 cup vegetable oil
3. One pound potatoes, peeled and cubed
4. One tsp salt
5. 1/2 tsp cayenne pepper
6. 1/2 tsp ground turmeric
7. 1/4 tsp ground cumin
8. 2 tomatoes, chopped

DIRECTIONS:

1. Grab a frying pan or skillet to begin. Add some oil to your skillet and begin to brown some onions.
2. Once onions are nicely brown season them with the following: cumin, salt, turmeric, and cayenne.
3. Combine with the seasoning your potatoes, and cook everything for at least ten mins. Make sure that you are stirring consistently as you do not want your seasonings to burn.
4. After ten mins has elapsed, mix in tomatoes and allow everything to cook until the potatoes are soft.
5. The pan should be covered and the cooking time for this step is about ten mins.
6. Allow everything to cool.
7. Serve.

Serving Size: 4 to 6 servings

Preparation	Cooking	Total Time
10 mins	20 mins	30 mins

Nutrition Information:

Calories	235 kcal
Carbohydrates	25.7 g
Cholesterol	0 mg
Fat	14.1 g
Fiber	4 g
Protein	3.3 g
Sodium	593 mg

* Percent Daily Values are based on a 2,000 calorie diet.

Tandoori I

Ingredients

1. 2 pounds chicken, cut into pieces
2. One tsp salt
3. One lemon, juiced
4. One 1/4 cups plain yogurt
5. 1/2 onion, finely chopped
6. One clove garlic, minced
7. One tsp grated fresh ginger root
8. 2 tsps garam masala
9. One tsp cayenne pepper
10. One tsp yellow food coloring
11. One tsp red food coloring
12. 2 tsps finely chopped cilantro
13. One lemon, cut into wedges

DIRECTIONS:

1. Grab your pieces of chicken and begin to take off the skin.
2. For each piece of chicken you want to create a slit or cut from the top to the bottom.
3. Get a non deep dish and add some salt and lemon juice to the chicken pieces. Making sure to cover everything.
4. Allow everything to marinate for at least 20 minutes.
5. Grab some yogurt, onion, garlic, cayenne pepper, ginger, and masala, and combine everything in one nice sized bowl.

6. Combine and stir the contents until smooth. Add some yellow and red food coloring (or skip if you do not care for non natural ingredients)
7. Combine the yogurt based mixture with the chicken and allow it to marinate in a frig for at 6 hrs. But an entire day is ideal (24 hr).
8. Get an indoor grill grate or an outdoor grill and set to a medium heat level and coat it with oil or non stick cooking spray.
9. Place the chicken pieces on the grill and let them cook until the middle is no longer pink.
10. Remove from grill and garnish with lemon pieces and cilantro.
11. Plate and enjoy.

Serving Size: 4 servings

Preparation	Cooking	Total Time
25 mins	20 mins	1 day 45 mins

Nutrition Information:

Calories	356 kcal
Carbohydrates	13.7 g
Cholesterol	102 mg
Fat	18.8 g
Fiber	3.3 g
Protein	35.6 g
Sodium	734 mg

* Percent Daily Values are based on a 2,000 calorie diet.

GRILLED TANDOORI II

Ingredients

1. 2 (6 ounce) containers plain yogurt
2. 2 tsps kosher salt
3. One tsp black pepper
4. 1/2 tsp ground cloves
5. 2 tbsps freshly grated ginger
6. 3 cloves garlic, minced
7. 4 tsps paprika
8. 2 tsps ground cumin
9. 2 tsps ground cinnamon
10. 2 tsps ground coriander
11. 16 chicken thighs
12. olive oil spray

DIRECTIONS:

1. Get yourself a medium sized container for mixing the following ingredients: ginger, yoghurt, cloves, salt, pepper, and salt (a bowl would be ideal).
2. Also combine the following taking care to mix all the contents together evenly: coriander, garlic, cinnamon, paprika, and cumin.
3. Set this mixture to the side to settle and move on to the next step.
4. Grab your chicken and clean it under some water (ideally cold water).
5. After the chicken has been cleaned. Dry it with napkins or paper towels (apply a patting motion for best drying results).

6. Now you want to take your chicken and mix it with the yogurt mixture we made earlier. In a large plastic bag that is reseal-able. Make sure that after you have added the chicken and yogurt to the bag you remove all the air which will be trapped inside.
7. Work the bag by turning it upside down and shaking it lightly to evenly dispense mixture and cover all the chicken.
8. Put this bag of chicken in a container and place it in the frig for at least 8 hours (ideally you would allow this to marinate overnight) reposition the bag occasionally (not necessary but recommended).
9. Get your grill ready. Set it to a medium level of heat and cover the grate with oil or a non stick cooking spray.
10. Remove each piece of chicken from the bag and spray it with olive oil. Place it on the grill.
11. Allow each piece of chicken to receive direct heat for 2 minutes.
12. Then turn each piece of chicken and allow for direct heat for another 2 mins.
13. Move each piece of chicken to the side of the grill and let it receive indirect heat for at least 25 to 35 mins and make sure the internal temperature of the meat is at least 180 degrees Fahrenheit.
14. Remove from grill, plate, and serve.
15. Throw away the remaining seasoning left over in the bag.

Serving Size: 8 servings

Preparation	Cooking	Total Time
10 mins	45 mins	8 hrs 55 mins

Nutrition Information:

Calories	349 kcal
Carbohydrates	5.4 g
Cholesterol	120 mg
Fat	20.5 g
Fiber	1.1 g
Protein	34.2 g
Sodium	618 mg

* Percent Daily Values are based on a 2,000 calorie diet.

Tomato Chicken Indian Style

Ingredients

1. One large onion, chopped
2. 4 cloves garlic, chopped
3. One slice fresh ginger root
4. One tbsp olive oil
5. 2 tsps ground cumin
6. One tsp ground turmeric
7. One tsp salt
8. One tsp ground black pepper
9. 1/2 tsp ground cardamom
10. One (One inch) piece cinnamon stick
11. 1/4 tsp ground cloves
12. 2 bay leaves
13. 1/4 tsp ground nutmeg
14. 6 skinless chicken thighs
15. One (14.5 ounce) can whole peeled tomatoes, crushed

DIRECTIONS:

1. Plug in your food processor and place some ginger, onion, and garlic into it.
2. Turn the processor on and process these ingredients into a smooth mixture.
3. Next grab a frying pan or skillet, and add some oil to it. Heat the pan and the oil with a medium level of heat.
4. Once the pan and oil is heated grab your paste and combine it with the oil. Make sure to

constantly stir the paste and oil to avoid burning.
5. Let the contents cook for 10 mins.
6. Add to your paste the following ingredients: nutmeg, cumin, bay leaves, salt, cloves, pepper, cinnamon, and cardamom.
7. Combine and mix all the above ingredients making sure to stir consistently for about 2 minutes until you smell a good aroma of spice and seasoning.
8. Now grab your chicken pieces and combine them with the paste making sure they are evenly covered with the seasoning.
9. Combine and cook the new mixture for about 4 mins making sure you are continually stirring.
10. After 4 mins. Add tomatoes.
11. Lower the temperature of the heat to low and let everything nicely simmer for a few hours (ideally 2 hrs).
12. When you notice a splitting of the oil from the mixture begin to stir. Make sure you have the pan covered lest you will have to add water every once and a while.

Serving Size: 6 servings

Preparation	Cooking	Total Time
15 mins	2 hrs	2 hrs 15 mins

Nutrition Information:

Calories	134 kcal
Carbohydrates	6.9 g
Cholesterol	57 mg
Fat	5.4 g
Fiber	1.6 g
Protein	14.7 g
Sodium	547 mg

* Percent Daily Values are based on a 2,000 calorie diet.

KORMA

Ingredients

1. 1/4 cup cashew halves
2. 1/4 cup boiling water
3. 3 cloves garlic, peeled
4. One (1/2 inch) piece fresh ginger root, peeled and chopped
5. 3 tbsps vegetable oil
6. 2 bay leaves, crumbled
7. One large onion, minced
8. One tsp ground coriander
9. One tsp garam masala
10. One tsp ground cumin
11. One tsp ground turmeric
12. One tsp chili powder
13. 3 skinless, boneless chicken breast halves - diced
14. 1/4 cup tomato sauce
15. One cup chicken broth
16. 1/2 cup heavy cream
17. 1/2 cup plain yogurt
18. One tsp cornstarch, mixed with equal parts water

DIRECTIONS:

1. Grab a small container and combine the boiling water with cashews. Allow this mixture to sit for about 20 mins.

2. Get your food processor ready for work. Add garlic and ginger inside the processor and work the contents until they become a paste. Once the contents are a paste set it to the side.
3. Grab a skillet or wok and add some oil and get it nice and hot with some medium heat.
4. Add your bay leaves to the oil and let it cook. Bay leaves should fry for about half of a minute.
5. Now you should add some onion to the oil and fry them down until translucent (three to five mins).
6. Get your food processor contents (ginger and garlic) and combine it with the onions and let everything fry for five minutes.
7. Combine with the mixture the following seasonings: chili powder, coriander, turmeric, masala, and cumin.
8. Combine your chicken with the seasoning and fry it for five minutes. Now combine your chicken broth as well as your tomato sauce. Make sure that you cover this pot, and lower the temperature.
9. Let everything slowly simmer for 15 mins. Make sure to stir the contents every once and a while.
10. Grab that food processor again and throw in some cashews and their accompanying water into the food processor with some yogurt and cream. Mix it all together until paste like.
11. Now take your food processor mixture and combine it with the chicken let everything cook for another 15 mins.

12. Finally combine the cornstarch and let everything go for an additional 2 mins.
13. Let food cool.
14. Plate it. Serve it. Enjoy it.

Serving Size: 4 servings

Preparation	Cooking	Total Time
20 mins	40 mins	1 hr

Nutrition Information:

Calories	398 kcal
Carbohydrates	13.4 g
Cholesterol	95 mg
Fat	27.5 g
Fiber	2 g
Protein	25.3 g
Sodium	477 mg

* Percent Daily Values are based on a 2,000 calorie diet.

Spinach Dahl

Ingredients

1. One 1/2 cups red lentils
2. 3 1/2 cups water
3. 1/2 tsp salt
4. 1/2 tsp ground turmeric
5. 1/2 tsp chili powder
6. One pound spinach, rinsed and chopped
7. 2 tbsps butter
8. One onion, chopped
9. One tsp ground cumin
10. One tsp mustard seed
11. One tsp garam masala
12. 1/2 cup coconut milk

DIRECTIONS:

1. First step is to take your lentils and put them in a container filled with water for about 20 minutes (soak everything).
2. Grab a large pan, add some water, and boil it. Once the water is boiling combine the following ingredients: chili powder, salt, turmeric, and lentils.
3. Now you need to cover the pot and get it boiling again. Once you have the pot boiling immediately turn the temperature down to get a nice simmer going.
4. You want everything to simmer for approx. 15 mins. Now add your spinach to the simmering goodness and let it simmer and cook for

another five mins. At this point you should notice your lentils are nice and soft (if not continue simmering). Remember to add more water if you think it is needed.
5. Grab another pan. This time a smaller one.
6. Place the new pan over medium heat and combine the following ingredients: mustard seeds, melted butter, cumin, and onion. Make sure that you are stirring this mixture constantly.
7. Cook everything down until the onions are transparent. Once you find that your onions are transparent combine the mixture with the lentils from earlier.
8. Finally combine lentils with coconut milk, and garam masala.
9. Heat everything for a few more mins (2 mins).
10. Let contents cool.
11. Plate and enjoy.

Serving Size: 4 servings

Preparation	Cooking	Total Time
10 mins	30 mins	40 mins

Nutrition Information:

Calories	362 kcal
Carbohydrates	44.9 g
Cholesterol	15 mg
Fat	13.4 g
Fiber	18.3 g
Protein	21 g
Sodium	693 mg

* Percent Daily Values are based on a 2,000 calorie diet.

Masoor Daal

Ingredients

1. One cup red lentils
2. One slice ginger, One inch piece, peeled
3. 1/4 tsp ground turmeric
4. One tsp salt
5. 1/2 tsp cayenne pepper, or to taste
6. 4 tsps vegetable oil
7. 4 tsps dried minced onion
8. One tsp cumin seeds

DIRECTIONS:

1. First step when dealing with lentils is to clean them. So run the lentils through water until the water runs clear.
2. Grab a sauce pan and place your clean lentils in it with the following seasonings: cayenne pepper, ginger, salt, and turmeric.
3. Take all these ingredients and submerge them in water inside of your sauce pan. Get everything to nicely boil. Make sure that you remove any foam which manifests during the boiling process.
4. Lower the temperature and let the contents simmer. Make sure you stir everything every once and a while.
5. Let the food simmer until the lentils are nice and soft and everything looks like a soup.
6. Grab a container that can be put in the microwave. Inside of the container place the

following things: cumin seeds, oil, and dried onion.
7. Set the container in the microwave on the highest setting for 45 secs.
8. Get the onions to a brown like color but make sure to not burn them.
9. Take out the microwave contents and combine it with the lentils.
10. Plate, serve, enjoy.

Serving Size: 4 servings

Preparation	Cooking	Total Time
5 mins	30 mins	35 mins

Nutrition Information:

Calories	185 kcal
Carbohydrates	25 g
Cholesterol	0 mg
Fat	5.2 g
Fiber	9.7 g
Protein	11.1 g
Sodium	868 mg

* Percent Daily Values are based on a 2,000 calorie diet.

Spicy Mango Chicken

Ingredients

1. 2 medium mangoes, peeled and sliced, divided
2. One (10 ounce) can coconut milk
3. 4 tsps vegetable oil
4. 4 tsps spicy curry paste
5. 14 ounces skinless, boneless chicken breast halves - cut into cubes
6. 4 medium shallots, sliced
7. One large English cucumber, seeded and sliced

DIRECTIONS:

1. Grab your blender and get it ready for some work.
2. Combine mango slices and coconut milk in the blender and blend it up until paste like. Place these contents aside.
3. Get a cooking pot and put some oil in it and heat everything with a medium level of heat. Once the oil is hot add your curry paste and let everything fry until you can smell a great aroma. This should take about one min.
4. Get the shallots and the chicken. Add these things to the curry oil and fry it all down until the chicken is fully cooked and your shallots are nice and soft. This should take about five mins of frying.
5. Grab your mango mixture from the blender and fry it down as well with the chicken and shallots.

6. Before serving add some more mango pieces and also some cucumbers.
7. Let cool. Enjoy.

Serving Size: 4 servings

Preparation	Cooking	Total Time
25 mins	10 mins	35 mins

Nutrition Information:

Calories	398 kcal
Carbohydrates	31.1 g
Cholesterol	58 mg
Fat	20.4 g
Fiber	3.3 g
Protein	26.5 g
Sodium	179 mg

* Percent Daily Values are based on a 2,000 calorie diet

Indian Style Eggplant

Ingredients

1. One eggplant
2. 2 tbsps vegetable oil
3. 1/2 tsp cumin seeds
4. One medium onion, sliced
5. One tsp chopped fresh ginger
6. One large tomato - peeled, seeded and diced
7. One clove garlic, minced
8. 1/2 tsp ground turmeric
9. 1/2 tsp ground cumin
10. 1/2 tsp ground coriander
11. 1/4 tsp cayenne pepper
12. 1/2 tsp salt, or to taste
13. ground black pepper to taste
14. 1/4 cup chopped fresh cilantro

DIRECTIONS:

1. For this recipe we will need the broiler. So turn on the broiler and get it hot before continuing.
2. Grab your eggplant and coat it with oil. You can also coat it with cooking spray.
3. Put the eggplant beneath the broiler and let it broil until it becomes soft and you notice the skin peeling off. This will take about 30 minutes. Make sure that you evenly cook the eggplant by turning it.
4. Grab a knife and halve the eggplant from top to bottom.

5. Remove the flesh from the vegetable. Throw away the skin.
6. Once the flesh of the eggplant has been removed dice it up and put it to the side.
7. Grab a frying pan or skillet and put oil in it. Get the pan and oil hot with a medium level of heat.
8. Once the oil is hot add some cumin seeds and let them fry for a bit. You should notice them turn brown but make sure that you do not burn them. While oil is still hot add the following: garlic, onion, and ginger.
9. Make sure that you stir and cook everything until tender.
10. Next combine with the onions your tomatoes and the following other seasonings: black pepper, turmeric, salt, cumin, cayenne and coriander.
11. Let these cook while stirring for a few minutes (2 mins)
12. Now we are ready for the eggplant.
13. Combine your eggplant dices with the frying spices and let it fry until you notice a good amount of the moisture has been removed. This should take about 15 mins.
14. Taste the eggplant and add more seasonings if you so desire.
15. Let the contents cool.
16. Plate and serve. Enjoy.

Serving Size: 4 servings

Preparation	Cooking	Total Time
15 mins	50 mins	1 hr 5 mins

Nutrition Information:

Calories	119 kcal
Carbohydrates	13.4 g
Cholesterol	0 mg
Fat	7.4 g
Fiber	6.1 g
Protein	2.4 g
Sodium	300 mg

* Percent Daily Values are based on a 2,000 calorie diet.

Aloo Gobi

Ingredients

1. 1/4 cup olive oil
2. One medium onion, chopped
3. One tbsp minced garlic
4. One tsp cumin seeds
5. One (15 ounce) can diced tomatoes
6. One (15 ounce) can coconut milk
7. 2 tbsps ground coriander
8. One tbsp salt
9. One tbsp ground turmeric
10. One tbsp cayenne pepper
11. One tsp ground cinnamon
12. One tsp ground ginger
13. One tsp ground cardamom
14. 3 large Yukon Gold potatoes, peeled and cubed
15. One medium head cauliflower, chopped into bite size pieces
16. One (15 ounce) can garbanzo beans, drained
17. 2 tbsps garam masala

DIRECTIONS:

1. Get a nice sized pot and place it over a medium heat level with oil and onions. Fry the onions until they are translucent. This typically will take about four mins.
2. Once your onions are translucent then combine some cumin and garlic and continue frying the ingredients until you find your onions are turning a brownish color.

3. Now begin to mix in the following: cardamom, tomatoes, ginger, coconut, cinnamon, coriander, cayenne, salt, and turmeric.
4. Continue to cook the contents until they begin to boil. Once everything is boiling add the garbanzo beans, potatoes, and cauliflower. Take care to mix everything well.
5. Now it is important to lower the cooking temperature to low and place a lid on the cooking pan.
6. Allow everything to simmer nicely until you notice the potatoes are soft. This will take about 45 mins to an hour.
7. Once the potatoes are soft add some garam masala and stir.
8. Let the mixture cook for an additional five mins before serving.
9. Enjoy

Serving Size: 4 servings

Preparation	Cooking	Total Time
10 mins	1 hr 20 mins	1 hr 30 mins

Nutrition Information:

Calories	622 kcal
Carbohydrates	64 g
Cholesterol	0 mg
Fat	39.2 g
Fiber	14.9 g
Protein	13.1 g
Sodium	2172 mg

* Percent Daily Values are based on a 2,000 calorie diet.

CURRY SHRIMP

Ingredients

1. 2 tbsps peanut oil
2. 1/2 sweet onion, minced
3. 2 cloves garlic, chopped
4. One tsp ground ginger
5. One tsp ground cumin
6. One 1/2 tsps ground turmeric
7. One tsp paprika
8. 1/2 tsp chili powder
9. One (14.5 ounce) can chopped tomatoes
10. One (14 ounce) can coconut milk
11. One tsp salt
12. One pound cooked and peeled shrimp
13. 2 tbsps chopped fresh cilantro

DIRECTIONS:

1. Grab a large frying pan or skillet. Place the pan over a medium heating level.
2. As always, add some oil, and some onions.
3. Let these onions cook until you find that they are translucent. This will occur in about four mins.
4. Once the onions are ready take the skillet from the stove and place it to the side for about two mins.
5. Now add the following ingredients to the onions: chili powder, garlic, paprika, ginger, turmeric, and cumin.

6. Place the pan back over a low heating level. Making sure that you are continuously stirring everything.
7. With the pan over a low heat. Add coconut milk and tomatoes and salt to the seasoning. Let everything begin to simmer nicely. Make sure that you stir the contents every once and a while. This simmer process should last for about ten mins.
8. Now add shrimp, with dried and fresh cilantro, to your simmering mixture and let it continue to simmer for another minute or so.
9. At this point the food is ready for serving.
10. Enjoy.

Serving Size: 4 servings

Preparation	Cooking	Total Time
15 mins	15 mins	30 mins

Nutrition Information:

Calories	416 kcal
Carbohydrates	10.9 g
Cholesterol	146 mg
Fat	32.1 g
Fiber	2.9 g
Protein	23 g
Sodium	930 mg

* Percent Daily Values are based on a 2,000 calorie diet.

Curry Fish

Ingredients

1. For the marinade:
2. 2 tsps Dijon mustard
3. One tsp ground black pepper
4. 1/2 tsp salt
5. 2 tbsps canola oil
6. 4 white fish fillets
7. One onion, coarsely chopped
8. 4 cloves garlic, roughly chopped
9. One (One inch) piece fresh ginger root, peeled and chopped
10. 5 cashew halves
11. One tbsp canola oil
12. 2 tsps cayenne pepper, or to taste
13. 1/2 tsp ground turmeric
14. One tsp ground cumin
15. One tsp ground coriander
16. One tsp salt
17. One tsp white sugar
18. 1/2 cup chopped tomato
19. 1/4 cup vegetable broth
20. 1/4 cup chopped fresh cilantro

DIRECTIONS:

1. Get a non deep dish for mixing. Combine the following in this dish: 2 tbsps of canola oil, mustard, half a tsp of salt, and some pepper to taste.

2. Now grab the fish pieces and place them into the mixture and make sure to evenly coat them. Place the fish in the frig for at least 30 mins.
3. Now grab a food processor and get it ready for some work.
4. Place the following items into the food processor: cashews, onion, ginger, garlic.
5. Process everything into a nice smooth paste.
6. Place this paste aside for a moment.
7. Now let's get the oven ready.
8. Turn the oven on to 350 degrees Fahrenheit or 175 degrees Celsius for preheating.
9. Now grab a nice frying pan or skillet and heat it up with a medium heating level with one tsp of canola oil.
10. Grab that paste we made earlier and mix it with the hot oil. Make sure to cook and stir the paste and oil for about two mins.
11. Now combine the following ingredients into the paste for seasoning: sugar, cayenne pepper, one tsp of salt, turmeric, coriander, and cumin.
12. Allow these seasoning to fry for about 5 mins making sure to stir as well.
13. Now grab your veggie broth and diced tomatoes and mix them into the seasonings.
14. Take out your fish and place them on a dish for the oven.
15. Throw away any left-over marinade.
16. Use our seasoning in the pot to coat the fish and let everything cook in the oven for about 30 mins.
17. To determine if your fish is ready grab and fork and see if the fish easily flakes. If so you are ready to garnish it with some cilantro.

18. Plate for serving.
19. Enjoy

Serving Size: 4 servings

Preparation	Cooking	Total Time
20 mins	35 mins	1 hr 25 mins

Nutrition Information:

Calories	338 kcal
Carbohydrates	11.6 g
Cholesterol	56 mg
Fat	13.5 g
Fiber	2.3 g
Protein	41.6 g
Sodium	2715 mg

CHICKEN BIRYANI

Ingredients

1. 4 tbsps vegetable oil
2. 4 small potatoes, peeled and halved
3. 2 large onions, finely chopped
4. 2 cloves garlic, minced
5. One tbsp minced fresh ginger root
6. 1/2 tsp chili powder
7. 1/2 tsp ground black pepper
8. 1/2 tsp ground turmeric
9. One tsp ground cumin
10. One tsp salt
11. 2 medium tomatoes, peeled and chopped
12. 2 tbsps plain yogurt
13. 2 tbsps chopped fresh mint leaves
14. 1/2 tsp ground cardamom
15. One (2 inch) piece cinnamon stick
16. 3 pounds boneless, skinless chicken pieces cut into chunks
17. 2 1/2 tbsps vegetable oil
18. One large onion, diced
19. One pinch powdered saffron
20. 5 pods cardamom
21. 3 whole cloves
22. One (One inch) piece cinnamon stick
23. 1/2 tsp ground ginger
24. One pound basmati rice
25. 4 cups chicken stock
26. One 1/2 tsps salt

DIRECTIONS:

1. Okay let's begin this recipe by grabbing a frying pan or large skillet and mix in some veggie oil (two tbsps).
2. Once our veggie oil is hot add potatoes and fry them until they are a brownish color.
3. Once the potatoes are brown remove any excess oil and place them to the side for work later.
4. Keep the pan hot and add two more tbsps of oil and add some garlic, onion, and ginger.
5. Cook these contents until you find that your onions are nice and soft and slightly brown.
6. Now we want to add the following ingredients to our onions for seasoning: tomatoes, chili, salt, pepper, cumin, and turmeric.
7. Make sure that you vigorously stir the seasonings to protect them from burning while frying for about five mins.
8. Now we want to combine the following ingredients: a cinnamon stick, yogurt, cardamom, and mint.
9. Once these ingredients are added we want to place a lid over the pot and lower its heat to the lowest level.
10. Take care to stir the mixture every once and a while until you find that the tomatoes have been turned into a pulp.
11. You may notice that the mixture will become dry and sticky. If this is the case you will need

to combine some hot water to the cooking pot occasionally.
12. Once the contents are thick. Grab your chicken pieces and combine them with the sauce.
13. You will want to make sure to mix the chicken well with the sauce so that every piece is evenly coated.
14. You now want to place a lid on the mixture and lower the temperature to its low level.
15. The chicken should be heated at this level while covered until you find that it is tender. Typically this will take about 35 to 45 mins.
16. Cook the chicken down until you notice a bit of gravy left. If you find that the gravy is too much remove the lid from the cooking dish for a while and let the contents continue to cook.
17. Now let's get to the rice.
18. Get your rice and wash it until you find the water running clear. Drain the water with a colander and let the rice sit aside for about thirty mins.
19. Now grab a large frying pan or skillet and add some veggie oil with some onions and fry it up until it is nice and golden.
20. Grab the following ingredients and add them to the onions: rice, saffron, ginger, cardamom, cinnamon stick, and some cloves. Make sure that you stir consistently until you find that your rice is completely covered with spice.
21. Now we need to get another pot of a medium size.
22. Grab some chicken stock as well as some salt.

23. When you find that the rice is nice and hot you want to add this chicken stock and salt to it. Make sure that you combine everything well.
24. Now let's grab that chicken and potato pot from earlier.
25. We want to combine the chicken and potatoes nicely into the rice mixture.
26. Cover the rice pot with a lid and make sure it is completely sealed. We now want to take the temperature down to its lowest level and let this rice simmer for about 20 mins.
27. Make sure that you do not lift the lid while it is cooking.
28. After 20 mins has elapsed remove the lid and fluff the biryani.
29. It is now ready to be plated and served.
30. Enjoy.

Serving Size: 6 to 8 servings

Preparation	Cooking	Total Time
≈ 30 mins	≈ 1 hr 30 mins	≈ 2 hr 30 mins

Nutrition Information:

Calories	832 kcal
Carbohydrates	78.9 g
Cholesterol	134 mg
Fat	35.1 g
Fiber	5.1 g
Protein	47.8 g
Sodium	1522 mg

* Percent Daily Values are based on a 2,000 calorie diet.

BROWN RICE, CHICKEN, CURRY, CASSEROLE

Ingredients

1. One cup water
2. One (8 ounce) can stewed tomatoes
3. 3/4 cup quick-cooking brown rice
4. 1/2 cup raisins
5. One tbsp lemon juice
6. 3 tsps curry powder
7. One cube chicken bouillon
8. 1/2 tsp ground cinnamon
9. 1/4 tsp salt
10. 2 cloves garlic, minced
11. One bay leaf (optional)
12. 3/4 pound skinless, boneless chicken breast halves - cut into One inch pieces

DIRECTIONS:

1. First we need to get our oven ready. So let's turn it on to 350 degrees Fahrenheit or 175 degrees Celsius for preheating.
2. Now grab a frying pan or skillet and combine the following: bay leaf, water, garlic, stewed tomatoes, salt, brown rice, ground cinnamon, raisins, bouillon, lemon juice, and curry powder.
3. Get everything nice and hot so it is boiling.
4. Once we find our mixture is boiling we want to add chicken to it.

5. Now make sure to stir the chicken into the boiling mixture and then move all of the contents to a baking dish (preferably a casserole dish)
6. Finally we want to place a lid on the baking dish and place it into the oven for about 45 mins. Making sure that we occasionally stir the contents.
7. Eventually we will find that the rice is tender and the chicken is fully cooked. In which case this is ready for plating and enjoyment.

Serving Size: 4 servings

Preparation	Cooking	Total Time
15 mins	1 hr	1 hr 15 mins

Nutrition Information:

Calories	241 kcal
Carbohydrates	34.5 g
Cholesterol	50 mg
Fat	2 g
Fiber	3 g
Protein	22.7 g
Sodium	620 mg

* Percent Daily Values are based on a 2,000 calorie diet

ALOO MATAR

Ingredients

1. 1/4 cup vegetable oil
2. 2 medium onions, finely chopped
3. One tbsp ginger garlic paste
4. One bay leaf
5. 4 large potatoes, peeled and chopped
6. One cup frozen peas
7. 1/2 cup tomato puree
8. One 1/2 tsps garam masala
9. One 1/2 tsps paprika
10. One tsp white sugar
11. One tsp salt
12. 2 tbsps chopped cilantro

DIRECTIONS:

1. Grab a wok and some oil and get them both hot and ready for cooking before going to the next step.
2. Once we have a hot wok grab the following ingredients and add them to the wok: bay leaf, onions, garlic paste, and ginger.
3. Make sure to fry the seasonings while stirring consistently until you find that the onions are translucent.
4. Once the onions are see-through and ready. Combine peas and potatoes with your onions.
5. Place a lid on this pot and let it cook down until the potatoes are soft. Typically this will take about 15 mins.

6. One you find that the potatoes are soft discard the bay leaf.
7. Grab the following ingredients to mix in: salt, tomato puree, sugar, garam masala, and paprika.
8. Combine everything and let it all cook for about 10 minutes.
9. Finally we want to grab some cilantro and throw it in. Let everything go for about another 2 mins and it is ready for serving.
10. Enjoy.

Serving Size: 4 servings

Preparation	Cooking	Total Time
15 mins	30 mins	45 mins

Nutrition Information:

Calories	487 kcal
Carbohydrates	81.7 g
Cholesterol	0 mg
Fat	14.5 g
Fiber	9.7 g
Protein	9 g
Sodium	898 mg

* Percent Daily Values are based on a 2,000 calorie diet.

POTATOES INDIAN STYLE

Ingredients

1. 3 tbsps ghee
2. One tsp cumin seeds
3. One tsp turmeric
4. One tsp ground coriander
5. One tsp salt
6. 1/2 tsp mustard seed
7. 1/2 tsp ground cayenne pepper
8. 6 medium potatoes, peeled and diced
9. 2 cups water
10. One cup yogurt
11. 2/3 cup frozen green peas

DIRECTIONS:

1. Grab a frying pan or a skillet and get some veggie oil as well. Place the oil into the pan and place everything over a medium level of heating.
2. Get everything nice and hot and add the following ingredients: cayenne pepper, cumin, mustard seed, turmeric, salt, and coriander.
3. Get your potatoes and put them into the frying pan as well. Be sure to mix everything well and make sure you coat the potatoes with veggie oil or ghee.
4. For about one min make sure you consistently stir everything and let it cook down nicely.
5. After 10 mins of stirring and cooking combine water into the frying pan.

6. After the water has been added lower the heat to its lowest level and let everything simmer for about 30 mins. At which point you should notice your potatoes are soft.
7. Once the potatoes are soft add some yogurt and peas into the mix and make sure everything is heated nicely before cooling.
8. Plate.
9. Enjoy.

Serving Size: 4 servings

Preparation	Cooking	Total Time
15 mins	45 mins	1 hr

Nutrition Information:

Calories	396 kcal
Carbohydrates	64.7 g
Cholesterol	28 mg
Fat	11.3 g
Fiber	8.6 g
Protein	11.3 g
Sodium	677 mg

* Percent Daily Values are based on a 2,000 calorie diet

Dahl II

Ingredients

1. One cup red lentils
2. 2 tbsps ginger root, minced
3. One tsp mustard seed
4. 2 tbsps chopped fresh cilantro
5. 4 tomatoes, chopped
6. 3 onions, chopped
7. 3 jalapeno peppers, seeded and minced
8. One tbsp ground cumin
9. One tbsp ground coriander seed
10. 6 cloves garlic, minced
11. 2 tbsps olive oil
12. One cup water
13. Salt to taste

DIRECTIONS:

1. Before anything we need to get our lentils nice and soft. So grab a pressure cooker and add the lentils.
2. Pressurize them until they are soft. Otherwise cook the lentils in a pot with water (slower method).
3. Grab a frying pan or skillet and get some oil hot with mustard seeds as well.
4. You'll notice the mustard seeds begin to flutter when the oil is very hot. This is what we are looking for.

5. When the mustard seeds are fluttering add the following ingredients: garlic, onions, jalapeno pepper, and ginger.
6. We want to stir fry all these ingredients until both the garlic and onions are nice and brownish.
7. Once the onions are brown and golden add some cumin and coriander to the mix.
8. Continue by adding tomatoes.
9. Stir fry the contents until you notice the tomatoes are done. Add some water at this point.
10. Let the newly added water begin to boil for about six mins.
11. Now we need to combine the cooked lentils with some salt with the boiling mixture.
12. Finally combine some cilantro before serving the dish right off the heat.
13. Enjoy.

Serving Size: 6 servings

Preparation	Cooking	Total Time
≈ 30 mins	≈ 1 hr	≈ 2 hr

Nutrition Information:

Calories	209 kcal
Carbohydrates	30.6 g
Cholesterol	0 mg
Fat	5.7 g
Fiber	12.7 g
Protein	10.4 g
Sodium	

* Percent Daily Values are based on a 2,000 calorie diet

OKRA CURRY

Ingredients

1. 4 cups okra, cut into 1-inch pieces
2. One tbsp olive oil
3. One tsp cumin seeds
4. One onion, chopped
5. 2 tomatoes, diced
6. One tsp curry powder
7. One tsp salt

DIRECTIONS:

1. First we need to grab a dish that can be microwaved safely.
2. Grab your okra and put it into this dish, which should be as large as possible.
3. Cook the okra in the microwave for about six mins on its highest setting.
4. Now find a frying pan or skillet and add some cumin seeds and olive oil.
5. The oil and seeds should be placed over a medium level of heat and eventually you'll notice them begin to swell.
6. Once cumin seeds have begun to swell take the onion and begin to fry it.
7. The cooking process of the onion should last for about three mins.
8. After the onions have been cooked grab your tomatoes and add them to the mix.
9. Allow the tomatoes to cook for three more mins.

10. After the tomatoes have cooked for a bit we need to combine our tomatoes with the okra, some salt, and some curry powder.
11. Finally stir the contents for about three mins at which point it is ready for plating.
12. Serve and enjoy.

Serving Size: 4 servings

Preparation	Cooking	Total Time
20 mins	15 mins	35 mins

Nutrition Information:

Calories	100 kcal
Carbohydrates	15.8 g
Cholesterol	0 mg
Fat	3.9 g
Fiber	5.3 g
Protein	3.4 g
Sodium	597 mg

* Percent Daily Values are based on a 2,000 calorie diet

Lentil, Tomato Soup, Indian Style

Ingredients

1. One onion, finely chopped
2. One tbsp olive oil
3. One chili pepper, chopped
4. One cup red lentils
5. One (14.5 ounce) can peeled and diced tomatoes
6. One cup water
7. salt and pepper to taste
8. 1/2 tsp ground cumin
9. One tsp dried basil
10. 1/4 cup sour cream
11. 2 fresh basil leaves

DIRECTIONS:

1. Grab a pan for heating possibly a Dutch oven. You want to begin heating some olive oil in it.
2. Once you have the oil heated add some onions and cook them down until they are translucent.
3. Once the onions are translucent we want to add the following ingredients: basil, tomatoes, cumin, chili pepper, and lentils with some water.
4. All the contents should be brought to a boil.
5. Once everything is boiling you must lower the heat to a low to medium level and put lentils.
6. Once at the low to medium level let everything simmer nicely for about 20 mins. At this point you will find that the lentils are soft.

7. Now that the lentils are ready we should take a stick blender and mash the soup until it has been nicely pureed. You can now add some salt and pepper if you like but it is not necessary.
8. Serve and enjoy.

Serving Size: 4 servings

Preparation	Cooking	Total Time
5 mins	25 mins	30 mins

Nutrition Information:

Calories	239 kcal
Carbohydrates	32 g
Cholesterol	6 mg
Fat	7 g
Fiber	11.1 g
Protein	12.8 g
Sodium	269 mg

* Percent Daily Values are based on a 2,000 calorie diet

Indian Style Salsa

Ingredients

1. 4 cups chopped tomatoes
2. 2 cups green bell pepper, chopped
3. 3/4 cup chopped onion
4. One cup jalapeno pepper
5. One 1/2 tsps salt
6. 1/2 tsp minced garlic
7. One 1/4 cups cider vinegar

DIRECTIONS:

1. Grab the following ingredients and combine them in a nice sized pot: vinegar, bell peppers, garlic, onion, salt, and hot peppers.
2. Heat the contents until it begins to simmer nicely.
3. Once you find that the mixture is simmering place a lid over the pan and let it continue to simmer for about an hour.
4. The longer you allow the salsa to simmer the spicier and tastier it will be.
5. When suited to your taste. Let the mixture cool and serve.
6. Enjoy.

Serving Size: 6 servings

Preparation	Cooking	Total Time
5 mins	1 hr	1 hr 5 mins

Nutrition Information:

Calories	56 kcal
Carbohydrates	10.5 g
Cholesterol	0 mg
Fat	0.6 g
Fiber	3.2 g
Protein	1.9 g
Sodium	971 mg

A Gift From Me To You...

I know you like cultural food. But what about Japanese Sushi?

Join my private mailing list of readers and get a copy of *Infinite Sushi: A Complete Set of Sushi and Japanese Recipes* by fellow BookSumo author Hashimoto Kazuma for FREE!

http://booksumo.com/classical-indian-cooking-simple-indian-recipes/

Enjoy some of the best sushi available!

You will also receive updates about all my new books when they are free. So please show your support.

Also don't forget to like and subscribe on the social networks. I love meeting my readers. Links to all my profiles are below so please click and connect :)

Facebook

Twitter

Google +

Come On...
Let's Be Friends :)

I adore my readers and love connecting with them socially. Please follow the links below so we can connect on Facebook, Twitter, and Google+.

Facebook

Twitter

Google +

I also have a blog that I regularly update for my readers so check it out below.

My Blog

About The Publisher.

BookSumo specializes in providing the best books on special topics that you care about. *Classical Indian Cooking: Simple, Easy, and Unique Indian Recipes* will take you on a journey to India with simple and easy dishes.

To find out more about BookSumo and find other books we have written go to:

http://booksumo.com/.

CAN I ASK A FAVOUR?

If you found this book interesting, or have otherwise found any benefit in it. Then may I ask that you post a review of it on Amazon? Nothing excites me more than new reviews, especially reviews which suggest new topics for writing. I do read all reviews and I always factor feedback into my newer works.

So if you are willing to take ten minutes to write what you sincerely thought about this book then please visit our Amazon page and post your opinions.

Again thank you!

INTERESTED IN MY OTHER COOKBOOKS?

Check out some of my similar cookbooks on different cultural food like:

Egypt, Morocco, Persia, & Pakistan:

Arabia & Asia: A Cookbook with Recipes from Egypt, Morocco, Persia, & Pakistan

Lebanon:

Classical Lebanese Cooking: Simple, Easy, and Unique Lebanese Recipes

Persia:

A Kitchen in Persia: Classical and Unique Persian Recipes

Made in United States
Troutdale, OR
05/29/2024